Porcelain Boy

Poems of bipolar disorder

Martin Hansen

& Katie Suponch

Porcelain Boy

Poems of bipolar disorder

Porcelain Boy
© Martin Hansen & Katie Suponch, 2019

Translation of the Danish book "Porcelænsdreng"
Martin Hansen is a pseudonym

Translation assistance & cover design: Katie Suponch
"Mummified Intrusion" illustration by Katie Suponch

Publisher: BoD – Books on Demand,
Copenhagen, Denmark
Prodution: BoD - Books on Demand GmbH - Norderstedt, Germany
ISBN: 9788743008231

1. edition

you grabbed my feet in my early youth, when the world was lying open to me. you built an obstacle course and you threw me in the middle.

initially i went off course but i could still navigate through the obstacles. i was puzzled about the bumps but i did not give them any meaning, because i still managed to hold on to the many things, which gave me quality of life. but you grabbed me and had no intention to let go.

you became more demanding through the years and your course became harder to navigate through. you blocked the door to the exits and you filled the course with alcohol and pill abuse. when you opened the door again, i had lost the will to live and i tried to leave the world. you could not accept that, so you threw me at the hospital where i lived for a long period of time.

i fought back. i fought myself out of the alcohol fogs and out of the pill's sedating effect. i found a small pocket in life, in which i could navigate without your interference. you still tried to control my life but i kept you away. i fought you and i took small steps and i tasted momentary victories. your obstacle course appeared from time to time, but i could find my way out most of the time.

you still have a firm grip on my feet, but i accept your presence. i live with your limitations.

i live with you.

symptoms

in the garden

green grass on unhardened feet
sun on bent shoulders
i am sitting in my parents' garden
counting yellow flowers

the redcurrant bushes
multiply as they shall
the potato crop has failed
there is a window missing
in the greenhouse

i do not worry
about all those things
worry about the chaos
that surrounds
my head

porcelain boy

porcelain boy
i stand on the shelf
squinting
vigilant
in disguise

glass fish
i take punches
obey orders
from soldiers
in the yard

white stripes
on my cheeks
territory markers
pipe dreams

clay pigeon
my thoughts are flowing
dreams about wings
outstretched arms

porcelain boy
i stand on the shelf
gather dust

another brick

concert
with pink musicians
we sit in orchestra pits
beer in plastic cups
gloaming time
in the outskirts

police present
law enforcers
they open pockets
confiscate herbs

i hold friends
in weary hands
shout familiar words
against a screen
of cloth

i close my eyes
throw thoughts overboard
tears against stained grass
i cannot see through
my darkness

supermarket

friday afternoon
in a blue supermarket
shopping with little cash
i smell olive oil
taste fruit

thoughts in boxes
breathe peace
breathe quiet
pleased with things
and conditions

change of scenery
chemistry in bones
adrenaline in fragile legs
speed driver
racehorse

i parry voices
from tiny grocer
noise in my head
from too much listening

i lean against
a pallet of juice
pass through pile of boxes
towards the exit
and leave

amusement park

ferris wheel
swings crooked
for my eyes
green treetops
with withered leaves
descend against my face
flashing lights
mixed high pitch noises
in my ears
will not let go

i follow
acquaintances
meet trouble
halfway

road

the road to the abyss
is wide
i am at the top
gaze at tree crowns
point at birds

two steps forward
i count grass
on telemeters
made of plastic
too far between them

shiny cars
behind me
drive too fast
too long
still people
by my side
lawless

the road to the abyss
is wide
i take two steps
back

psychiatrist

i visit
a psychiatrist
she tells me
to slow down

i do not understand
everything she says
her clothes are too dirty
for my healthy outer

she gives me medication
it is supposed to help me
when i get nervous
it does not
help me

i am sitting on her couch
trying to understand
why i feel so bad

trees

i climb trees
make noises with bells
in a green crown

look down too long
see the filthy dirt
below the grass

belt around my waist
hooks in my arms
frost bursts on my fingers
they call for warmth

weather above my head
snow in my lungs
can't breathe
i throw my anchor
on a weak branch

withered feet
bloodshot cheeks
i want to go down

bus

back seat
in a yellow bus
ticket in my hand
sliding door shut
behind me

alien mother
with alien child
large hand in small
green stuff on narrow seat
next to her

old man
with no teeth
scolds himself
and everybody
the disability seat
is not for healthy people

young man
sits beside me
communicates with his friends
he has cheap dirt in his mouth
smells of beer

i keep an eye on the display
tells me when to stop
wishing me away

anxiety

chase
through unknown streets
feet firmly floating
transparent concrete
i am in third gear

i change direction
run across the street
with recklessly
closed eyes
and back again

soundless attack
i tank up courage
to fight back
i can only hear
my own voice

chase
i cannot put myself on hold
i am at my own heels

psychologist

psychologist with round glasses
lives in a sterile room
kleenex and decanter
plastic cups upside down
books on ugly shelves

comfortable chair
i lean back
put my face in fetal position

armor made of sheet metal
on my chest
velvet gauntlets
on my hands
i am trapped in the metaphor jungle
without a dictionary

psychologist with round glasses
movie director
scriptwriter
hollow punches in pillows
powerlessness
in my arms

on the road

buildings bite the dust
before my hands
foreign soil
before my arms
airport dust
below my feet
dry crumbs
in my mouth

i see dragons
on distant walls
dogs run
without keepers
the air is filled
with plastic

a ride on four rims
dirt road
against alien recesses

i run with flour in my mouth
do not care about the
consequences
could not care
less

bar

the bar is packed
i am drunk
with intentions
think too little

drinks on the counter
my mouth is filled
with smooth words
and crooked sentences

red color on the ceiling
euphoria on the dance floor
fixed stares
in weary faces
without eyes

exchange of gazes
hunting season
with a rifle
and scents in a bottle

ugly bitches
are the easiest
ask no questions
just come along

i am the king
of the night

bitch under my arm
too easy

psychiatrist #2

i pull out needle marks
from my sleeves
i shout in pillows
talk with noise
in my mouth

not familiar
with the doctor words
my ears are not grown up
yet
i close them
pretend to understand

i talk to closed doors
rubble on my voice
sound against open sky
i leave the clinic
without answers

in the forest

i lie down
look at tree tops
gaze at squirrels
with claws
on their feet

my thoughts
are filled with speed
refueling on a stone
in the forest

i listen to fallen leaves
on my face
green colors
on yellow worries

i have brought
a sleeping bag
too sick
to return
to my life

rest stop

portable rest stop
just a small detour
with rapid breath
yellow car draws streaks
paints circles

engine inspection
on tarnished asphalt
measurable downfall
written in capitals on stained concrete

maintenance check
social meltdown
and career in corroded drains
a free fall without parachute
endless risks
without beginnings

oil change
white powder in plastic pills
two in the mouth without water
for safety precautions

portable rest stop
darkened rims on yellow car
terminal velocity
with rapid breath
and back in traffic

left behind

left behind
in the outskirts of the world
held prisoner
by feelings
in free fall
against deep recesses
in my mind

left behind
by woman
carpets torn from the wall
lamps on the floor
without glow

left behind
no passion for life
buckled up
by tears
to my ears
restrained
by the past

interview

i greet
shake too many hands

no limit for
achievements and
distinctions
i have collected autographs
from the best players
on the pitch

eye contact
across a green table
false promises
and large expectations
i put my light
under a bushel

smile from the other side
two next to each other
maybe too wide
if you ask me
but no one does

hotel

planes behind my window
before my eyes
killers in the night
milk human blood

monsters in depressions
behind bars
i drink coffee
without filter

sport stars
on the run
i need epo

i step out of the bed
turn the telly off
close the door
to my room
cut out
noises

new year

last day of the year
streamers on the wall
hair confetti
mask on me

my faces
make scenes
for my friends

jack daniel's in the guest room
painkiller
lifesaver
for the next hour's
torment

dinner with courses
from the bottom of the sea
joy around the table
laughter in the bushes
i smile crookedly
with genuine concern

cigarette break
marlboro in spacious back garden
firm grip in the backpack
i swallow two benzodiazepines
with a glass of wine

rockets
prophecies in the sky
i need clairvoyance
to see
what they say

anxiety #2

noise
down the road
i try to slip away
run with flashing lights
in my hands

bare footed
crown on my head
white robe
flies to another side
when i move my toes

convulsions
i cannot run anymore
have to crawl
instead

darkness

coffee table with hardened stains
couch on my back
paste on my sweater
i am chained to green cloth
with black coating

darkness before my face
hard to see straight
heavy thoughts
in heavy mind

loneliness attack
my mouth moves
talks to the people
who are not there

computer on my lap
forbidden fluid in my veins
i am living room depressed
cannot live
anymore

on the way

blue hazard flashers
on yellow houses
i have lost sense of direction
the ambulance has turned left
too many times

accelerated sentences
between two paramedics
radio contact to the hospital
i do not understand
what they yell about

porter under my arms
helps me to my bed
quilt with blue letters
will not fold

fuss in the hallway
nurses in all directions
demons dancing on the ceiling
midnight performance
hose in my stomach
looking for pills
i throw up
upon the lettered quilt
and the clean floo

hurricane

belt

pills blow up my mouth
i refuse to swallow
a firm grip around my neck
i don't pay attention

threats and admonitions
recoil on my armor
i am the king of this facility
i discharge pills
shout with blood in my mouth

four hands on my shoulders
two legs locked
one clean floor on my chin
three hags on my back

achromatic room
with colored bulb
it shines a light on my sedated body
the belt tightens my stomach
i want to go home

force

sedated patients
in one-way corridors
doctors with sharpened needles
electricity in their fingers

staff under my arms
my hands turn upside down
vote fishers
abusers

cup with white powder
sedates my soul
i cannot move it
anymore

king's chair
too many parts in my legs
canceled leave of absence
and back to the ward

visit

visit from girlfriend
date behind closed doors
under supervision

she still doesn't like
to be frisked
at all

i promise her
that i only will be manic
in my own ward
from now on

hear tears fall to the floor
i collect them
they run through my fingers

maybe i didn't hold on
tight enough

mania

i evade divinity
and warlords
in the hospital corridor
staff on my back
tries to grab my heels
my legs move too fast
they can't get a grip

laughter from the air ducts
a scent of foreign languages
on my tongue

slow patients
queue on the hospital corridor
i jump over the checkered floor
in lack of pace

i lock myself in
the community room
i put a hot chair
in front of the door

captured and pacified
back in red ward
i throw medicine on the floor
and i fall apart

visit #2

visiting time is over
my parents walk around the corner
a always sad
decrease of sound

traffic in the corridor
heavy steps in heavy mind
my feet move
in no particular
direction

staff on the floor
white clogs in pace with
unopened pill bottles

i lie down on my bed
alone in my ward
gaze at a grey spot
on the concrete ceiling

yearn
miss
pray

social worker

a meeting in my cell
social worker with bun in her hair
mom and dad with worried glances
at my hands
i am cold and warm by turns
look at birds with beaks on the window
blanket on darkened sky

i listen to shallow words
with a needle in my arm
admonitions against armor
made of cloth
call to a manic mind

thoughts on retreating
my lonesome army
just words in my ear

sentences without meaning
hurl at my body
like dew from a dried-up sky

i said goodbye
close the door to my cell
i am king of the hospital
my home for a while

behind the door

door locked
window half open
my bed moves
through the ward
the wheels creak
beneath me

i scratch concrete
from crackled walls
quilts on floor
with grey linoleum
prevent free passage

i sit on my bed
straight up
i see too well
awake while dreaming

i listen to the noise
from the other side of the door
nurses talk
knitting recipes
slimming diets
i do not want to be in my ward
do not want to be here
i want to go home

flipping places

home again
medicine in my bag
direct line to the hospital
i can sleep in a safe environment
if i want to

i smell like hospital
cannot wash it off
because i don't take a shower

wine in the cupboard
this is the special occasion
i drink from the bottle
my lips turn blue
the vintage was not so good
anyway

i am not ready
to come home
i realize that
now

pub

i cross the street
with firm steps
rain is pouring down
draws streaks
of yellow people
on the curbs

pub on the corner
a decoy from home
just for a while
until the rain has stopped

i am high
on dopamine
low
on almost everything else

i am always the center
of gazing eyes
i have to sit down
on a vacant chair

loads of ugly women
i pick the second best
take off
into the afternoon

endlösung

pills in patterns
on the table
lithium in rows
in piles
dull color on the sky
darkness in my mind
angular thoughts
in empty bottles
grey stripes in grey hair
draw streaks
on shadowy hours
whiskey in cold blood
blends with rusty liquid
i am ready

back once again

doors with circular windows
close behind me
with numerous bangs
they lift the elevation bed
from the grey linoleum

i roll down the corridor
doors on both sides
i greet manic people
in a manic
state of mind

fantastic ideas
in fast thoughts
i am unable
to tie a knot
on them

boring ward
hand on reeled window
i dream myself back to the town
with an ambulance
in the fast lane

national hospital

darkness on the hospital floor
emptiness behind closed doors
i touch colored streaks
signposts

patient on the floor
staff on her back
she cries for help
abuse in broad daylight
i walk on

yellow light in the corridor
narrow cells on both sides
soundproof doors
psychosis under lock and key

lunch in the canteen
anorectic
and three times jesus
cock-and-bull stories
tortuous voices
i return to my ward
still hungry

my bed has wheels
i sit on the guest chair
keep myself company

i pray to god
to remove the black flies
that live in my mouth

perhaps he listens
another time

in my ward

darkness in my ward
demons fight
behind a hasped window
i sing songs of sorrow
for a locked door

staff in the corridor
heavy steps on polished concrete
personal attack alarms
and wrinkled shirts
surveillance

pieces of mania
repeat before my eyes
i lift my hands
fend out punches
i shout in the dark

i am defenseless
restless
alone

night at the hospital

springs against my back
wheels below the bed
i watch my dreams
on a white divider
yell at psychosis
in the ward beside mine

dreamcatchers on the ceiling
i count shadows
dance with my eyes closed

four windows
the lowest are locked
i can't fall out
and i can't run away

footsteps in the corridor
night watchman with bulletproof vest
i lie with my eyes closed
and my ears sharpened

peace and quiet at the hospital
sound of a pulsating heart
in my chest

voices

thin voices in green pipes
increase in volume
i hold someones hands
for my ears
i know the voices are not real

single ward in big hospital
i hear only sporadic traffic
nurses with buns
push checked tables
with unspecified medication

increasing voices
crack my armor
i fight with filter bags
on my bloodshot hands

smoke on the floor
leaks from a locked closet
i throw my body
from the elevation bed
i am the extinguisher
the problem solver

voices in my head
i have run out of responsibility
i sit on the guest chair
close my eyes and pull the cord

in the night

i sit on my elevation bed
my head is where my feet
are supposed to be

i gaze at the wall
with blind eyes
rubble and cracks
in armored concrete

smell of illness
in my ward
cordial on the table
untouched plate
knife and fork crossed
on my breast

there is no sound
from the grey linoleum corridor
the doctors have gone home
to withered lawns
the nurses have gone home
to the moon

the section has been shut down
the hospital is now at night
i do not know what day it is

ward door

the door to my ward
have snapped
the nails in the frame
bristle in every direction
poor quality

there is a free passage
to the grey linoleum corridor
standardization of prisoners

i stand in the opening
watch out for big screws
count traffic
and psychosis

i look in the one-way traffic
with lazy eyes
take small steps
on grey linoleum

apparently
i have become so well
that i can go home
to stay
for good

released

i put away my demons
in fourteen blue air ducts
i empty my dusty locker
for almost anything

i say my goodbyes to the staff
drink a cup of coffee
in the room with smoke

i give a last interview
to the doctor with the brown blazer
he updates my journal
for now

my parents are in the waiting room
bring along hope and a lift
i sit in the children's seat
distribution of roles

home

german series on the telly
pizza trays on the floor
my transmission is stuck
in first gear

pills in dispenser
on the dinner table
i must remember to eat
one extra blue pill

piles of laundry
next to the shower cabinet
toilet in the corridor
luxury problem

my apartment has been stagnant
while i was committed
now it won't move

alcohol

bottles on the table
in my pocket
i make fun of myself
of my shadow
not so alive anymore

racing thoughts
smelting of joy
i have a party
on a green couch
too far away
from anyone

tunnel vision
superficial gaze
at eight walls
occasionally too narrow

glass and bottle
on the table
i eat garlic
if guests show up
contrary to expectation

lithium

half empty lithium bottle
on the coffee table
jack at the end
of my arm
i swallow pills
drink in competition
with myself

uninhabited apartment
almost no furniture
in my living room
there is a diamond lighter
on my table

light from the pulse of the street
is stopped by curtains
which my father didn't hang up
my demons dance
on the naked floor

i lie down on the green couch
fold my arms
think thoughts
about death

relaxation therapist

pedagogue
puts fingers with stress relief
on my hips
strapped down on a blue floor
there is no escape
the chains on my arms
will not let go off my skin
i look at black hair
dyed

loose parts
heavy movements
can not pinch
tattered thoughts

the floor feels cold
on my chin
i close my eyes
put acts
away

district

my friend from the district
has no bun in her hair
i realize that now
as i go to pay her a visit

morning appointment
so i do not have to be without alcohol
for too long
i shake without bag-in-box wine

benzodiazepine on the counter
admonitions in my right ear
exit out the left
medicine addiction
not my problem

she smiles
see you tomorrow
i say my goodbyes
the street
is full of life
i hate mine

group therapy

intensions to the right
to the left
i am never in the middle

meanings around me
ungraceful song
from a bring along stereo
timer on overtime

powerpoint
from the eighties
with stained windows
i pull my last ringlet
of grey hair

i swallow impotence
look for escape routes
below the table
forced
to be in a room
with sick people
i count minutes

in the night

cracks in my thoughts
obstruct passage of dopamine
i get up from the bed
soaked with sweat

kitchen with dirty service
does not wash up spontaneously
i pour coca cola
with too much sugar

i sit on the green couch
remote points at telly
points at me
sedation of thoughts

cold living room floor
soothes my urge to move
hasn't been washed
for a long time

back in my bed
on the right side
on the left
i am my own arch-enemy
in the night

social services

council corridors in rows
narrow doors with green numbers
fates with hollow eyes
look at the pictures behind me

social worker with round glasses
and platinum blond hair
my destiny is sealed
with insisting keystrokes
legalist
keeper of laws

i play my card
bipolar disorder
i cannot work
but i have to

i hold my mother's hand
on our way to the car
too many chances
to fail again

anxiety #3

urge to move
my green couch is in the way
for sudden movements
firm steps
to the kitchen
back again

spider
on white wallpaper
writhes to the smoke
pulls five legs back

urge to create
pencil on blue squares
my dining table is full of
discarded paper

stomach convulsions
choke of medicine
i speak with my mouth full
cough black

recovery

wine

tuesday morning
in front of the supermarket
nine minutes until the doors open
my bones are cold
i squeeze bags
with empty bottles

three customers in the shop
decadent in sound
and appearance
i know where the wine rack is
value for money

i hide from clerks
and prejudice
three colored coins on the counter
and back on the streets

snow on the sidewalk
passengers on bikes
pedestrians in cars
i am cold to the bone
without wine

my kitchen is packed
with vacant stuff
i empty the bag from the supermarket
open bag-in-box wine

get ready to throw up
for a couple of hours

psychiatrist #3

i visit my psychiatrist
a monthly necessary evil
a ride with my dad
i do not know the way

sixteen steps to recovery
i take my father's hand
begin the climb

demons in my bag
over my shoulder
follow me when i walk
when i crawl

perspiring psychiatrist
with curved helmet
is late
we wait in the room
with all the posters
of healthy people

blood test answer
lithium too high
lamotrigine too high
cholesterol too high
i need to step down my medicine
and my mood

always the same message
it will never get any better
destroyer of hope
extinguisher of candles
i slam the door shut
will not see him again

solitary

bob dylan breathes over
his own shoulder
from his space on the wall
nicotine stains around the frame
two plants drop dead leaves
on grey floor
made of wooden boards

fighting next door
coptic words to my ears
i cannot understand
what they are yelling

i put on my walking boots
walk from kitchen to living room
and back again
i count footsteps
too much space
in my tiny apartment

phone without buttons
shiny glass without scratches
it cannot ring
apparently
it must be broken

i turn off the pulse of the street
with mission curtains

i defrost my meal
watch telly
until i go to bed

psychiatrist #4

engine inspection
at new psychiatrist
he wears a white lab coat
lives in a hospital
no nonsense
straight to the matter

big hospital
seems smaller
i do not live in my ward
anymore
but i am back
for a short amount of time

mood adjustment
new psychiatrist with white lab coat
adjusts my medicine
chemistry teacher
blood hound

lithium in my blood
is mixed with a cheap drug
two portions to one

i say goodbye
to new psychiatrist
i hope my medicine is working
this time

change of scenery

i think i can feel
that my medicine is working
just a bit
because i haven't felt like this
since i was very young
it is a much appreciated
transformation

bottle

green bottle
filled with fermented death
transparent liquid
flows from the center
brings destruction
along the way

green bottle
has caused disunity
in my family

green bottle
has made the days brown
opaque
ugly

green bottle
do not tempt me
any longer
i do not want it
in my life

heavy rocks

heavy rocks are lifted
from my weary body
put to rest
in the light of the biolamp
incinerated
by the fingers of pharmacology
silence arrives
like a thief in the night
and freedom has a sweet taste
on my salty tongue

home safely

footpath
in the outskirts of town
i thread snow steps
on my way home
throw rocks
from my chest
against the towers

supernumeraries with white veils
are brought alive
bicycles without lights
on enlightened road
hazard flashers
without batteries

front door
polished knob
made of imitated brass
opens inwards
light on the floor
in my home

living room

coffee in a flat cup
quiet living room
no movement
in green bolsters

liquid on the floor
paddling pool for bare feet
oil for chilled mind
dwindling ground water
in protected cups

stereo collections
on wooden shelfs
i pick songs
put them in the ground
with plastic spoons

i am
mould breaker
noise filter
alive

psychiatrist #5

my psychiatrist
has given me new pills
i do not care
that they are bad
for my body
they are good
for my mind

balance

balance
thoughts on a straight line

i am in the heart of my living room
my drying rack is full of clothes
in all sizes
i have washed it
myself

my couches have covers
from an expensive store
black streaks on old armrests
new life for old material

plants on the windowsill
green stalks against the light
life creator

my job is on a roll
a niche in the eleventh hour
sickness benefit cancelled
sense of stability

my hands are still shaking
i do not mind any longer
i am in balance

at work

open-plan office on the first floor
collegial noise through my ear
out the window
a way out
half open

my desk has one-way traffic
pencils and thoughts
checked paper in squares

community around me
laughter and job satisfaction
around me
i hide behind untold words

young colleagues
i am too old for them
sprinters
speeders
i wonder when to tell my boss
that i am sick

woman

unknown woman
a face of binary numbers
i form words with soft keys
dream in capital letters

unknown woman
behind my screen
luminous keys
below my fingers
sentence structure
without direction

unknown woman
listen to music
in mono
i dream in several colors
bleed blue blood
from my hands

unknown woman
without face
without expectations
on my mind

presentation

swift hands
cling to papers
cannot separate them
breathing is a completely
different issue

boss on my neck
fahrenheit in my nose
bad breath on my chin

sweat in my eyes
cannot see straight
my fingers tremble in step

shining keys
on laptop
i aim
cannot write straight

spectators on top of each other
fill corners
throw hands
at me

i listen to the applause
feel that i am alive
that I know
how to live

courage

she sits on the other side
of the compartment
reads heavy book
her eyelashes blink in time
with the music
in hear ears

i know i am not ready
my skeletons are still
holding my hands
i am not ready
but i know
that i will fall in love
the same moment
i brace myself

so i will do just that

mug

coffee mug
on wooden windowsill
terrazzo jars
filled with fertilizer
and soul
solar collectors along the curtains
draw twisted lights
give movement
to clasped hands
movable pieces
of alabaster stone
youth
to aging shell
decreasing shadows
on painted floor
and chequered mind

coffee mug
in my oasis
my home

field trip

field trip in the city
i have my hand
in her hands
we move to the city pulse
collect atmosphere

blue sky above the clouds
drips oxygen on our hair
i keep myself a small step
behind her
get seduced

we talk about nothing
laugh of it all
i enjoy every moment
of our twilight hour
in the city

mood chart

tiny smileys
on black background
i type with trembling fingers

coffee on the table
red mark on the cup
a manic warning
i promise myself
to be careful

there is a lot of rectangular objects
in my living room
i notice that now
as i type
circular objects are not in vogue
in my life

guitar from loudspeakers
green branches to the window
turned east
i smile
as i type
tiny smileys

date

hand under my arm
the sun is shining on the movie screen
moons on the curtain
her numb words on my chin
soft vowels

coffee under a cloudless sky
behind glass
my espresso is tepid
precious liquid

hand in hand towards the bus stop
her thoughts upon mine
a pocket of time
i enjoy it

white chocolate on the table
telly with dampened sound
too many legs in the couch
i move mine
lay myself close
to her

epilogue

i look back
recall hospitals
taste abuse
and failure

i look at the horizon
accept limitations
and possibilities
i live with them

world at my feet
instep kick
on rough surface
i place my ball
on the white mark

let the games begin